Volcanoes in time and space

Of the world's 500 or so active volcanoes, only a small proportion is in eruption at any one time, probably 20–30 in a year. An *eruption*, when the volcano gives off quantities of lava and volcanic gas, is usually of fairly short duration relative to the life of the volcano. A few volcanoes like Stromboli and the Hawaiian volcanoes are in more or less continuous eruption. But in the majority of volcanoes, there is a *dormant* period of relative inactivity between eruptions, when the volcano emits only minor quantities of gas and perhaps some lava, or of total inactivity, when it appears to be dead. The period of dormancy is usually much longer than the period of eruption, and may last tens of years or even thousands of years. A volcano which has not erupted in 'historic time' is said to be *extinct* but this designation is really extremely vague as 'historic time' may be much shorter than the period of dormancy. The 1973 eruption at Heimaey (fig 1) was unexpected; Helgafell, the only volcano on the island, had been dormant for about 5000 years and was considered extinct. Also, while 'historic time' may be several thousand years in some areas such as the Mediterranean, it is only a few tens of years in remoter parts of the world like Antarctica. It is probably wise to regard all Recent volcanoes (those that have erupted within the last 25 000 years) as potentially active.

With the exception of Australia, each continent has some volcanoes, although the geographic distribution within the continents is highly irregular (fig 54, pages 18–19). Volcanoes also occur in the oceans, initially as *submarine* eruptions, but eventually a volcanic island may form. Examples of this type of island are Tristan da Cunha in the Atlantic and the Hawaiian group of islands in the Pacific Ocean.

HJÁLMAR R.BÁRÐARSON

2 Faint sun shining through gas escaping from the lava lake, Surtsey, Iceland

J.E.GUEST

3 Sampling gas at Etna, 1971

What comes out of volcanoes

Volcanic gas

The molten *magma* which feeds volcanoes is a combination of lava and volcanic gas, with the gas held in the magma by the confining pressure inside the volcano. When pressure drops suddenly at the beginning of an eruption, the magma effervesces and gas separates out. The manner of separation governs the style and violence of an eruption; for example, gentle separation of gas and lava is seen in fig 2. Gases which commonly make up the gaseous mixture include water vapour, hydrogen, carbon monoxide, carbon dioxide, hydrogen sulphide, sulphur dioxide, sulphur trioxide, chlorine and hydrogen chloride in variable proportions. Measurement is hampered by the difficult physical conditions near an active vent and also because the gases react with the atmosphere and with each other, altering their composition and proportions. Asbestos-clad scientists in fig 3 are taking samples at an active gas vent on Mount Etna. The high temperature, about 1000°C, of the incandescent gas is vividly shown in fig 4, a night view of the same vent. Volcanic gas is released into the atmosphere and leaves behind little direct record of its eruption; however, gas is of great importance, and may play the dominant role in an eruption. For example, in the 1906 eruption of Vesuvius, gas was blasted from a 500 metre-wide crater with incredible force to a height of 13 km in a prolonged gas explosion which lasted 18 hours. This eruption reduced the height of the mountain by about 110 metres, leaving the crater enlarged to a diameter of 600 metres.

Lava

Lava eventually solidifies to rock and remains as a record of the eruption. The lava in fig 5a contains large white crystals which were formed in the magma prior to eruption; the brownish-grey groundmass crystallized shortly after eruption; and the irregular-shaped gas bubbles suggest this was part of a lava-flow of the type known as *aa* (a Hawaiian word pronounced 'ah-ah', see page 6 for explanation). The glassy lava in fig 5b was erupted as a partly-congealed, sticky, slow-flowing mass: such glassy lavas, like all glasses, are solids with the molecular structure of liquids. Had it been quenched suddenly, the crystalline lava would also have solidified to a glass: conversely, the glassy lava would have crystallized if it had cooled slowly at depth.

J.E.GUEST

4 A night view of the vent in fig 3

IGS

IGS

5 (a) Basalt, Edinburgh (b) Obsidian, New Zealand

Runny lava – almost always basalt – is very widespread both in the oceans and in the continents. The oceanic crust, beneath a thin layer of sediments, is made entirely of basaltic rock; this was erupted from long cracks which follow the crests of the mid-ocean ridges. The majority of isolated volcanoes in the oceans erupt lava of basaltic composition. Many continental volcanoes also emit basalt, and additionally, basalt is erupted in vast floods from fissures which penetrate the entire thickness (35–40 km) of the continental crust. The individual lava-flows of these *flood basalts* initially fill hollows in the ground surface, but after emission of many hundreds of flows, the land surface becomes a level plateau. The 700 000 cubic kilometres of flood basalts which make up the Deccan Plateau in India (fig 6) were erupted between 40 and 60 million years ago during India's northeastward drift from Africa to join the continent of Asia.

When first erupted, basalt is usually a very hot runny fluid: temperatures measured at basalt eruptions are quite commonly between 1100°C and 1200°C. Sometimes the surface temperatures of basalt may be even higher but this is usually attributed to the heating caused by burning of hydrogen and other volcanic gases as they escape from the lava surface. Near an active vent, basalt appears to bubble and flow quite freely: its 'stickiness' or resistance to flow (its *viscosity*) increases as the lava spreads from the vent and cools. The viscosity depends on several factors including the temperature and chemical composition of the lava, the amount and condition of dissolved gas, and the proportion of solid material (crystals or rock fragments) carried in the liquid.

The chemical elements contained in an average basalt are shown in fig 7. Although the most abundant elements are oxygen and silicon, these make up an even greater proportion of other kinds of lava. In general terms, the lower the proportion of oxygen and silicon, the less viscous is the lava; consequently basalt, with a relatively low proportion of these elements, is

6 **Lava-flows of the Deccan Plateau, India**

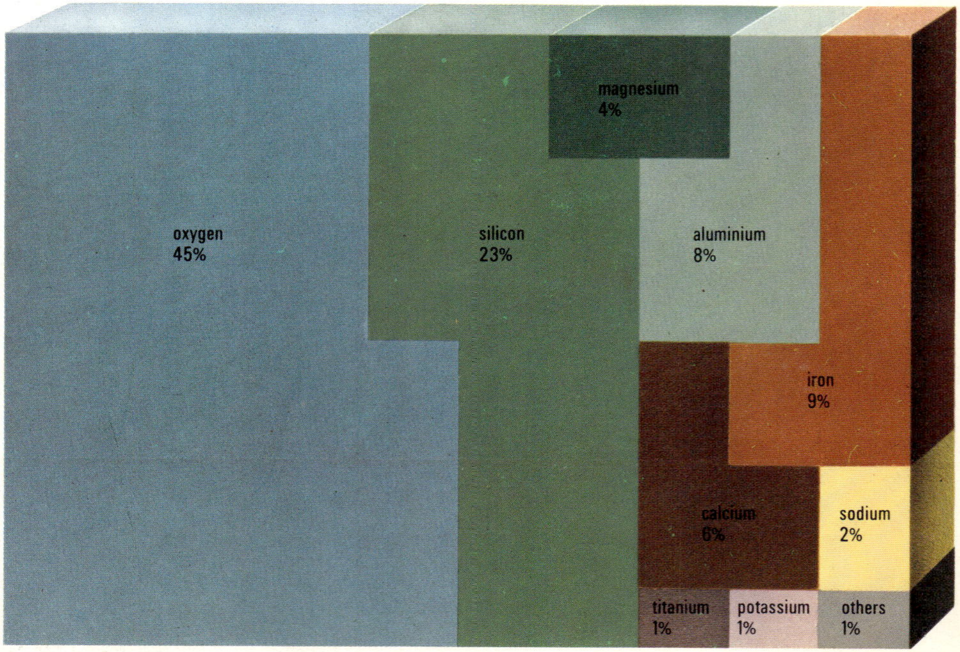

7 **The elements which make up basalt**

usually a very fluid runny lava. Because of this, basalt eruptions are normally not very violent and are therefore particularly suitable for close study and photography.

All magma before eruption is under hydrostatic pressure equal to the weight of overlying rocks. As it rises, gas separates as bubbles from the magma because the pressure is no longer sufficient to hold it in solution: in other words, the magma starts to froth. In hot basalt lava, the gas bubbles rise to the surface and escape easily from the runny fluid. If magma moves upwards slowly, the escape of gas is gradual and the eruption consists of gas emission followed or accompanied by gentle outpouring of degassed lava. If the rise is rapid however, frothing and escape take place simultaneously at the volcanic vent, and the eruption is more violent. Vigorous fiery fountains of red-hot lava may form over the vent: the fire-fountain in fig 8, photographed by night, is about 100 metres high, though fountains up to 500 metres in height have been observed at Hawaii (fig 9). The fountain in fig 10, photographed by day, shows the cooling and darkening of lava fragments during flight. The noise accompanying fountain activity has been likened to continuous dropping and smashing of crockery: the lava fragments chill during flight, and fracture on landing. If the lava is very runny, tiny droplets falling through the air trail threads of liquid behind them. These filaments, which are a common feature of some Hawaiian eruptions, are known as Pele's hair after Pele, the legendary goddess of Hawaiian volcanoes.

In fire-fountains the activity is more or less continuous, with variations in the height of the fountain. But in *Strombolian activity* red-hot lava fragments are hurled into the air by successive bursts of escaping gas, separated by short periods of quiescence lasting minutes or hours. This is the commonest type of activity at Stromboli, but also occurs at a great many other volcanoes. The time exposure of fig 11 has captured a Strombolian burst from the NE crater of Etna and shows the tracks of the lava fragments hurled through the air.

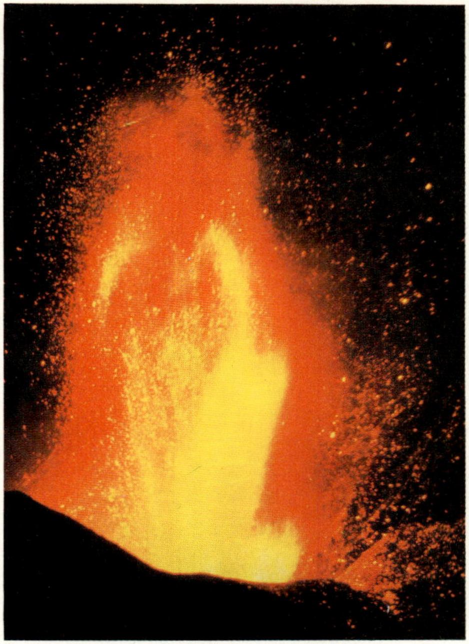
B.BOOTH

8 Lava fountain, Eldfjell, Iceland, 1973

G.A.MACDONALD, USGS

10 Lava fountain, Kilauea, Hawaii, 1955

WARD'S

9 Lava fountain, Kilauea, Hawaii, 1959

J.E.GUEST

11 Strombolian activity, Etna, 1970

Lava-flows

Some flows of basalt lava are very long, even when the ground slope is negligible: individual flows in the Columbia River plateau (USA) have lengths of about 200 km, and have spread out over almost horizontal ground. On the other hand, where the rate of emission of magma is low, tongues (flow units) of lava are shorter and pile up close to the vent, building a steep-sided cone like that of Fuji-san (Japan), a basaltic volcano (fig 38). Flows of what is assumed to be basalt lava have been observed on the Moon (fig 13).

Pahoehoe and *aa* are names used by Hawaiian natives to describe lava-flows with different surface features. The surface of pahoehoe is billowy and undulating with a smooth continuous skin; in fine detail, the skin is often covered in tiny spines and resembles sharkskin. The thin congealed skin remains plastic over the red-hot, fluid interior but may be tough enough to permit a man to walk across the moving pahoehoe-flow. Wrinkling of the plastic skin by flow movement causes the ropy structure which is a common, but by no means universal, feature of pahoehoe (fig 15). With thickening of the surface crust, lava may continue to flow internally in *lava tubes:* when the supply of magma slackens, the river of lava inside the tube subsides leaving a ramifying system of caves (fig 17). Aa-flows have an exceedingly rough surface layer of spine-covered, rubbly fragments (figs 14, 16). These flows are essentially rivers of lava which, at the front and sides, merge into thick banks of partly-congealed red-hot lava covered and underlain by rubble (fig 12). Fed from within by the lava rivers, the banks move slowly outwards, the fragments of rubble tumbling down the steep flow-front to be overridden by the advancing flow (fig 77).

There is apparently no chemical difference between pahoehoe and aa; indeed, pahoehoe may change into aa (but never the reverse) downstream, particularly where the lava plunges over a steep slope. Aa issues directly from the vent when magma is rather viscous, or if runny magma is agitated by fountaining at the vent. Gas bubbles or *vesicles* in pahoehoe are spherical in shape, whereas those in aa are irregular (fig 5a): this is due to differences in the rates of solidification and gas separation in the two types of lava. Vesicles may subsequently be filled in with mineral matter and these infillings are called *amygdales*. During cooling, massive, thick lava-flows develop cracks perpendicular to the cooling surface, the six-sided *columnar jointing* so well displayed at the Giant's Causeway in Northern Ireland, and on the Isle of Staffa. Thin lava-flows cool fairly quickly, but thick flows may take many years to cool. The flow in fig 14 was still hot to the touch after two months. A pool of basalt lava 100 m deep in Kilauea Iki Crater, Hawaii, had a solidified crust only 6 m thick after seven months.

G.A. MACDONALD, USGS

12 River of red-hot basalt lava feeding aa-flow, Kilauea, Hawaii, 1955

NASA

13 Lava-flows on the Moon, Mare Imbrium

14 Front of an aa-flow, Villarrica, 1971

16 Aa-flow pouring over cliffs of ash, Surtsey, Iceland

15 Ropy structure in pahoehoe, Surtsey, Iceland

17 Ropy pahoehoe in a lava tube, Mount Suswa, Kenya

Pasty lava, in contrast to runny lava, does not flow freely, and the high viscosity inhibits gas separation and escape; consequently eruptions look very different from those of runny lava. When the gas content is high, release of pressure causes violent explosive eruptions which may be heard great distances away (fig 104). When both the gas content and the pressure are low, pasty lava extrudes through the vent like thick toothpaste, forming volcanic domes (figs 18, 20). Fragments break or spall off the sides of the cooling lava and collect as *crumble breccia* around the foot of the dome. The upper surface of a dome is usually very irregular and may be covered with sharp extrusions of slightly hotter lava, called *spines,* which may grow to a considerable height, the highest recorded being 300 metres at Mont Pelée in 1902 (fig 114). Eventually, spines crumble away to a heap of breccia by continued spalling. Lava with a slightly lower viscosity spreads out round the vent as a very thick flow or a wide dome, the surface covered in smoothish blocks of lava, often so regular as to be almost cubic in shape. This *block lava* (fig 19) is sometimes regarded as a kind of aa, and in fact there is a complete gradation between the two. The extreme viscosity of silicon-rich lavas gives rise to horizontal jointing and small-scale lamination caused by shearing movement during flow; further flow may throw these horizontal structures into violent contortions. Some silicon-rich lavas that have cooled fairly rapidly before eruption are extruded in an almost solid condition as volcanic glass.

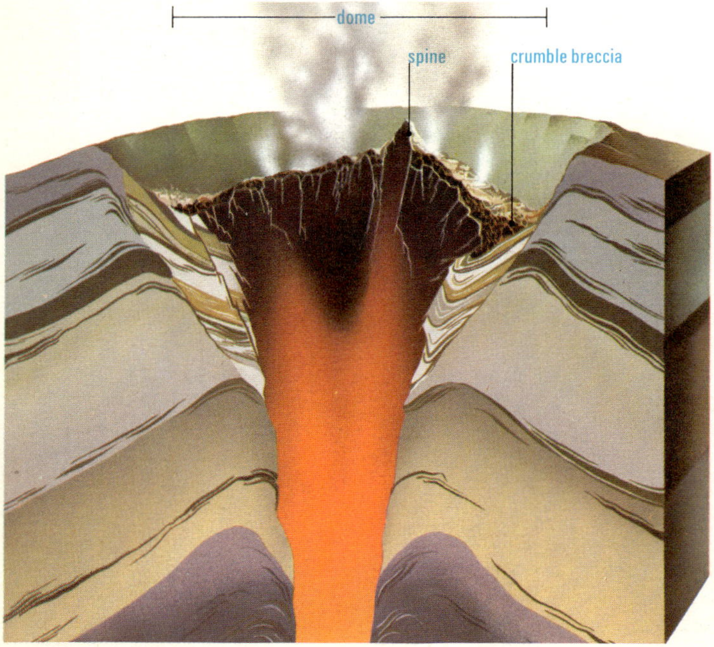

18 Growth of a dome and spine

G.A.MACDONALD, USGS

19 Edge of a block lava-flow, Lassen Peak, USA

J.E.GUEST

20 Lassen Peak, USA, a very large dome clothed in crumble breccia

Pumice is a lava so full of gas bubbles that it floats on water. It is produced by rapid frothing of viscous lava, caused by a sudden drop in pressure, but the bubbles once formed are unable to escape. Pumice usually forms from silicon-rich glassy lava, with each bubble separate from the next (fig 21). It may float for months on water and can be a serious hazard to shipping. Large rafts of pumice may explain reports of 'floating islands'. The specimen in fig 23 photographed with an equal weight of apples was erupted at Krakatoa in 1883 (page 34) and washed up some months later on the shores of Malagasy Republic. The less common basaltic pumice usually has interconnecting bubbles and quickly becomes waterlogged.

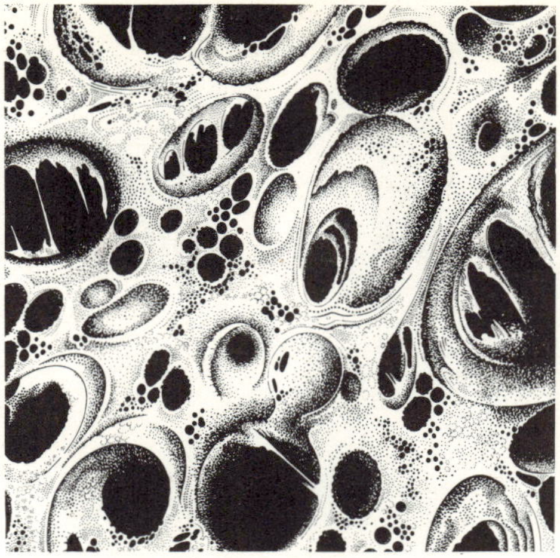

21 The texture of pumice in close-up

IGS

23 Pumice with an equal weight of apples

Ash-flows or *pyroclastic flows* result from frothing of magma in the vent, the gas bubbles expanding explosively, fragmenting the lava. A rapidly expanding emulsion of glassy lava fragments, crystals and gas spills out of the vent and flows downhill at speeds as high as 200 km per hour, eventually coming to rest as a dense blanket of hot lava fragments on the lower slopes of the volcano. This type of activity is called a *nuée ardente* or *glowing cloud*. Sometimes the explosion accompanying glowing clouds is directed upwards (fig 22) and the clouds sweep out in all directions. Occasionally an explosion in the crater propels a cloud sideways in one direction only. The glowing cloud eruption in fig 22 shows incandescent ground-hugging ash-flows visible on the right, while those on the left are obscured by turbulent clouds of fine ash. At Mayon in 1968 many glowing clouds were erupted, and these were scientifically observed and photographed. Eyewitnesses reported that the usual sequence of events was deep rumblings from the volcano, followed by vertical ejection of ash and blocks up to a height of 600 metres, from which grew an explosion cloud as high as 10 km. Tongue-like clouds emerged from the base of this vertical cloud and swept down the mountainside. In some eruptions, glowing cloud activity is

J.G.MOORE, USGS

22 Glowing cloud eruption, Mayon, Philippines, 1968

J.E.GUEST

24 **Columnar jointing in ignimbrite, N. Chile**

P.W.FRANCIS

27 **River gorge in ignimbrite, N. Chile**

P.W.FRANCIS

25 **Flame structure in ignimbrite, Tenerife**

G.P.L.WALKER

28 **Mud-flows at Fenais, Graciosa, Azores**

G.P.L.WALKER

26 **Looking towards Taal volcano from the devastated western shores of Lake Taal, Philippines**

accompanied by a highly destructive phenomenon: a rapidly-moving gas surge which precedes the main cloud. In the zone of maximum destruction, all standing objects are completely flattened; around this, trees are scoured, charred and stripped of bark on the side closest to the vent, but remain undamaged on the reverse side. In the 1965 eruption of Taal volcano, in Lake Taal in the Philippines, analogous effects were caused by surges of a different origin. This eruption took place on the lower slopes of the volcano and became highly explosive when lake-water gained access to the vent. Surges of mud suspended in steam spread out horizontally with hurricane velocity from the base of an explosion cloud 15–20 km high. Habitations on the shores of Lake Taal, about 5 km from the volcano, were devastated by the surges (fig 26).

Although the scientific terminology of glowing clouds and their rock products is controversial, most volcanologists would agree that glowing cloud activity gives rise to *ignimbrite,* the product of the ash-flow component, overlain by *air-fall ash*, the material which settles out of the turbulent cloud. Consolidated volcanic ash of all types is the rock called *tuff:* hence *ash-flow tuff*, roughly synonymous with ignimbrite. After deposition, ignimbrites may take many years to cool, particularly if the deposits are thick. The slow cooling promotes welding in the interior of the ignimbrite, with partial crystallization (devitrification) of the glassy fragments, a process aided by trapped hot gases and ground water. Fig 25 shows the welded portion of an ignimbrite with fragments flattened by compression during welding to produce the typical 'flame' structure. In close-up, most ignimbrites show Y-shaped shards of glass, the fragmental remains of the bubble walls. A conspicuous large-scale feature of ignimbrites is *columnar jointing* (fig 24), but this is less regular than in many lava flows, and the columns are commonly four-sided not six-sided. *Mud-flows* (sometimes called *lahars*) have killed more people and destroyed more property than any other type of volcanic activity in the last few centuries. Mud-flows (fig 28) are slurries of unconsolidated, unsorted volcanic debris lubricated by water, and they form in many ways. They may accompany an eruption, or they may form later after a heavy fall of rain or snow on new volcanic ash. Sometimes glowing clouds generate local tropical rainstorms which cause severe erosion of the snout of the ash-flow, producing mud-flows. Mud-flows also result from rapid melting of ice or snow on the volcano slope during an eruption. The speed and distance of mud-flows depend on local geography; speeds of up to 90 km per hour are recorded, and distances travelled are commonly 10–15 km though some mud-flows have travelled 180 km.

Snowdonia 450 million years ago was a group of low-lying volcanic islands surrounded by a shallow sea (fig 29). Glowing clouds, erupted from fissures on land and under the sea, were the dominant form of volcanic activity. Many of the ignimbrites in the area are not welded; presumably some of these were erupted under water (the submarine glowing clouds chill on contact with sea water and consequently are cold when they come to rest). There is an enormous variety of different volcanic rocks in Snowdonia, including lava-flows and fragmental deposits, of which some are ignimbrites, some mud-flows and some fragmental fall-out deposits. The magma which fed these volcanoes collected in underground blisters: these domed and cracked the overlying rocks which subsequently collapsed, leaving large depressions in the land surface which flooded with sea water. Compared with ancient ignimbrites, modern ignimbrites are paltry in size: the Valley of Ten Thousand Smokes eruption of 1912 in Alaska (p. 35) produced 28 cubic kilometres of ignimbrite, but in Triassic times (195–225 million years ago) an eruption in Queensland, Australia is estimated to have produced 2800 cubic km of ignimbrite in a few days. Extensive plateaux of ignimbrite such as those in northern Chile (fig 27) are presumed to have erupted from linear fissures.

29 Glowing cloud eruption in Snowdonia, 450 million years ago

G.P.L.WALKER

30 Explosive ashy eruption at a new crater on Etna

P.W.FRANCIS

31 Sloping layers of tephra, Las Canadas, Tenerife

Bombs, lapilli, and ash

The fragments of rock produced during volcanic explosions are called *tephra*. Explosions are caused by the sudden escape of volcanic gas trapped by congealed lava inside the volcano. The explosions may be small (fig 30), or they may be huge cataclysms greater even than the detonation of the largest hydrogen bombs. The explosion of Tambora in 1815, the largest historic volcanic eruption, was equivalent to 16 000 megatons, in comparison with the 0·02 megatons of the Hiroshima bomb. Prehistoric volcanic eruptions are estimated to have been many times greater than Tambora. Explosions may last several minutes or, rarely, many hours, as in the gas phase of the 1906 eruption of Vesuvius (page 3), which resembled the long-continued blast of a rocket.

Tephra may initially be old lava—the material that choked the vent after the previous eruption—but most tephra is new magmatic material. Fragments of non-volcanic rock, torn from the walls of the conduit by the ascending magma, are sometimes thrown out too. Tephra can be subdivided into small particles called *ash*, medium-sized particles (pea-sized to walnut-sized) called *lapilli*, and large particles called *blocks* or *bombs;* there is a complete gradation between these sizes. Ash, in spite of its name, is not a product of burning; it is pulverized lava composed of crystals, rock fragments or glass, or a mixture of all these. *Dust,* the very finest ash, sometimes travels great distances in the upper atmosphere, causing spectacular sunsets. Thick veils of dust in the atmosphere after violent eruptions may affect weather patterns. Blocks are ejected as solid fragments, while bombs are molten when thrown into the air; some bombs solidify during flight but others are still molten when they land. All bombs are modified by their flight through the air and form a variety of shapes depending on such factors as fluidity and the length of the flight path. Bombs of viscous lava acquire a glassy skin during flight which fractures on landing, allowing vesiculation of the interior; these are called *bread-crust bombs* (fig 37). Other shapes include *ribbon bombs* (twisted elongated strings), spindle-shaped *fusiform bombs, cow-dung bombs* (fig 33), and *spherical bombs.* An accumulation of bombs which were molten on landing is called *spatter* (fig 32); vesicular tephra which is solid when it lands is *scoria* or *cinder.*

Tephra accumulates around a vent in layers which thin out away from the vent, since most of the fragments and also the largest fragments fall close by. A cone made of sloping layers (fig 31) of tephra is built up round the vent. The finest particles may be distributed over a huge area: such ash layers are very useful in dating and correlating rocks, particularly where there are no fossils. Large bombs or blocks falling into unconsolidated ash will break or compress the ash layers, forming a *bomb-sag* (fig 35). The bomb in fig 36, thrown 200 metres from the fire-fountain in the background, has made a crater in the thin layer of scoria and has disturbed the turf underneath.

32 Spatter cones, from the porch of Hayashi House, Kilauea, 1955

G.A.MACDONALD, USGS

33 Cow-dung bombs, Kilauea, Hawaii, 1954

F.J.FITCH

34 Vegetation in Hawaii, six years after a cinder eruption

F.J.FITCH

35 Bomb-sag, 340 million years old, Eaglesham, Renfrewshire

IGS

36 Newly-formed bomb crater, Eldfjell, Iceland, 1973

I.FRIDLEIFSSON

37 Bread-crust bomb, Vulcano, ejected in 1888

G.P.L.WALKER

Shapes of volcanoes

The popular notion of a volcano is a graceful snow-capped cone like that of Fuji-san (fig 38). These cones, called *strato-volcanoes*, may, like Fuji-san, be composed almost entirely of lava-flows, in which the steep concave slopes are the result of many short flows piled one on top of another. Most typically, however, strato-volcanoes are built of layers of tephra, which thin away from the main vent, interbedded with lava-flows. *Shield volcanoes* (fig 39) are shaped like upturned saucers with very gentle slopes, between 2° and 10°. They are built by successive voluminous outpourings of fluid lava from a central vent, and include the largest volcanoes in the world. The Hawaiian Islands are the classic example of shield volcanoes: Mauna Loa, in the distance in fig 39, is the largest volcano of the group and is 100 km wide at the base and 10 000 metres high. The crater in the foreground of fig 39 is Kilauea, on the slopes of Mauna Loa. The symmetry and shape of both strato-volcanoes and shield volcanoes may be destroyed in the old age of the volcano by many factors, including *flank eruptions* which build small *parasitic cones* on the sides of the volcano, landslipping on steep slopes, sideways shift of the main lava conduit, collapse of the summit region, or a combination of these. A flank eruption on Tristan da Cunha, with an aa-flow spreading from a parasitic cone is viewed from above in fig 40, looking down onto the lava which is encroaching on the island settlement. A *scoria cone* or *cinder cone* (figs 41, 42) is a steep-sided cone built of sloping layers of unconsolidated scoria. During growth of a cinder cone or scoria cone, the volcanic activity may change, giving way to spatter activity so that a steeper rim of thoroughly welded spatter tops the scoria cone. The crater in fig 41, at the summit of such a scoria-and-spatter cone, has steep, scree-covered interior walls caused by avalanching of loose material after activity ceased. Beerenberg (fig 43) was initially a shield volcano, as shown by the gentle angle of the lower slopes, but more recently its activity has changed, lava heaping up around the vent to make a cone with a steeper slope. Volcanoes which erupt pasty lava vary in shape from steep-sided mountains covered in crumble breccia (fig 20) to groups of small rubbly domes which grow over fissures.

J.ALLAN CASH

38 Fuji-san from Shiznura, Japan

F.J.FITCH

39 Mauna Loa from Kilauea caldera, Hawaii

I.G.GASS

40 Flank eruption, Tristan da Cunha, 1962

J.E GUEST

41 Crater near Flagstaff, Arizona

G.P.L.WALKER

42 Montana Gorda from Sao Miguel, Tenerife

F.J.FITCH

43 Beerenberg, North Jan Mayen

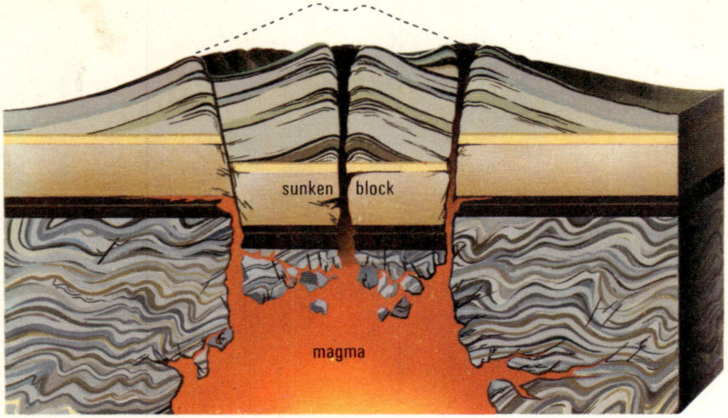

44 A caldera formed by block subsidence

In some calderas the rim is a circular *fault* (a fracture along which rock has slipped) which has allowed the middle portion to sink down as a block. The peripheral fault may grow spirally outwards so that the caldera gradually enlarges as the central mass subsides. The faulting, whether spiral or concentric, is probably caused by doming above the underground magma reservoir.

Calderas are volcanic craters larger than 2 km across, and they are particularly common on old-established volcanoes. Some calderas are formed by block subsidence (fig 44). Examples are the calderas Mokuaweoweo, 6 km by 4 km, and Kilauea (fig 39, foreground), 4 km by 3 km, in the Hawaiian Islands. The largest calderas are sited on ash-flow volcanoes and develop late in the history of the volcano, during a violent eruption which follows a lengthy period of dormancy, probably when the volcano has reached a critical size. It is popularly supposed that these volcanoes have 'blown their tops off', but the ash-flow products are new magmatic material. It seems that the underground magma reservoirs are emptied during eruption, and the summit of the volcano, having lost its support, collapses inwards piecemeal, leaving a *collapse caldera* or *explosion caldera.* The world's largest caldera, 23 km by 16 km is at Aso-san in Japan. At Tambora in 1815, a catastrophic eruption reduced the height of the mountain by 1400 metres, leaving a caldera 12 km in diameter. Trou au Natron, 1000 metres deep and 8 km in diameter, is a collapse caldera (fig 45) ; the white soda crust covering the floor of the crater is pierced by black volcanic conelets. The largest known volcano, Nix Olympica on Mars (fig 46), is a shield volcano 600 km in diameter with a composite summit caldera 65 km across.

A. PESCE

45 Caldera formed by piecemeal collapse, Trou au Natron, Tibesti, Chad

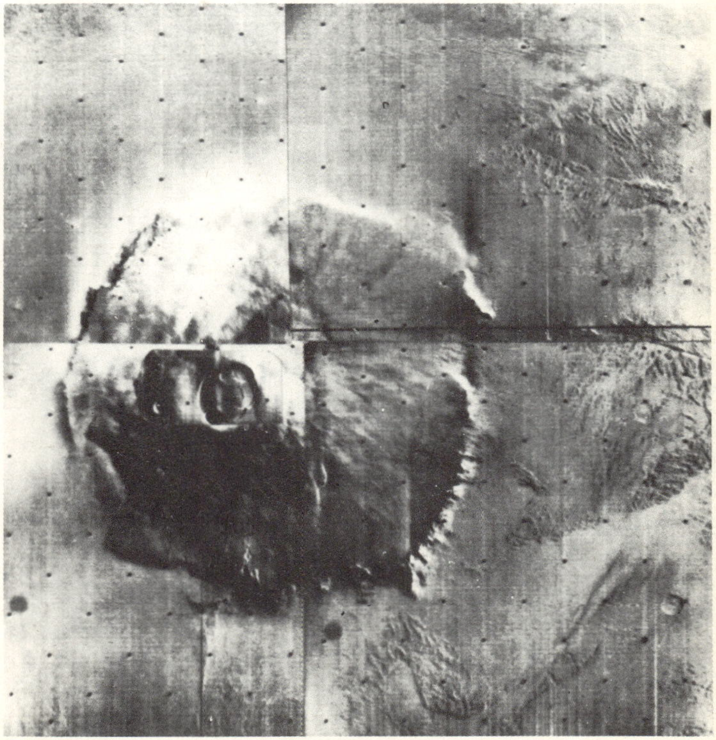

NASA

46 Shield volcano with summit calderas, Nix Olympica, Mars

Underwater eruptions

When lava is erupted under water (fig 47), it is rapidly chilled, forming a glassy, plastic skin around still-liquid lava. Bulbous shapes, called *pillows* (figs 48, 49), are formed in submarine eruptions, and also in eruptions under glaciers or where lava spills into a lake or marshy ground. Between individual pillows is a fine-grained glassy material, *hyaloclastite*, produced by shattering of hot lava on meeting cold water. Hyaloclastite reacts with water to form a brownish material, *palagonite*. Tephra which falls into water produces rocks with the textures of water-lain sediments; for example, size sorting of particles because of their different rates of fall through water causes *graded bedding* (fig 50), with the rapidly falling coarse fragments at the base of each unit grading upwards into fine material. Graded bedding and pillow structure can both be used to determine the 'way up' of ancient rocks: 'up' in fig 49 is to the left.

J.E.GUEST

48 Recent pillow lavas, Etna

H.TAZIEFF

47 Shallow-water submarine eruption, Fayal, Azores, 1957

IGS

49 Pillow lavas about 500 million years old, Ballantrae, Ayrshire

IGS

50 Graded beds in water-lain tuff (half-size), Haweswater, Westmorland

Fumaroles, hot springs and geysers

Fumaroles are vents which give off volcanic gases ranging in temperature from 100°C to 1000°C. Fumaroles can be the last waning phase of activity in an extinct volcanic area, but they are also found associated with both erupting and dormant volcanoes. Fumarole gases react with the surrounding rocks and atmosphere to produce minerals, often brightly coloured, which deposit around the vent (fig 51). Some fumaroles are magma gases, but others, the temporary fumaroles like those in the Valley of Ten Thousand Smokes in Alaska, originate in a cooling lava-flow or ash-flow which heats groundwater. Carbon dioxide is the main constituent of some fumaroles: this heavy gas accumulates close to the ground or in hollows as invisible asphyxiating death traps, like Death Gulch, Arizona. Groundwater heated by magmatic gas or hot surrounding rocks comes to the surface as *hot springs* and these are often associated with fumaroles. Some hot springs are bubbling pools of hot mud, sometimes brightly coloured. A *geyser* is a hot spring that ejects a fountain of hot water and steam at regular intervals, sometimes to considerable height. Waimangu in New Zealand was active between 1899 and 1904 and had a jet 500 metres high: it became inactive when the local groundwater level fell after collapse of a nearby natural dam. Geysers and hot springs (fig 52) commonly contain dissolved minerals which deposit around the vent, building fantastic terraces of *siliceous sinter* (fig 53).

P.W.FRANCIS

52 El Tatio geyser field, N. Chile

F.J.FITCH

51 Fumarole, White Island, New Zealand

T.M.THOMAS

53 Sinter terraces, Yellowstone National Park, USA

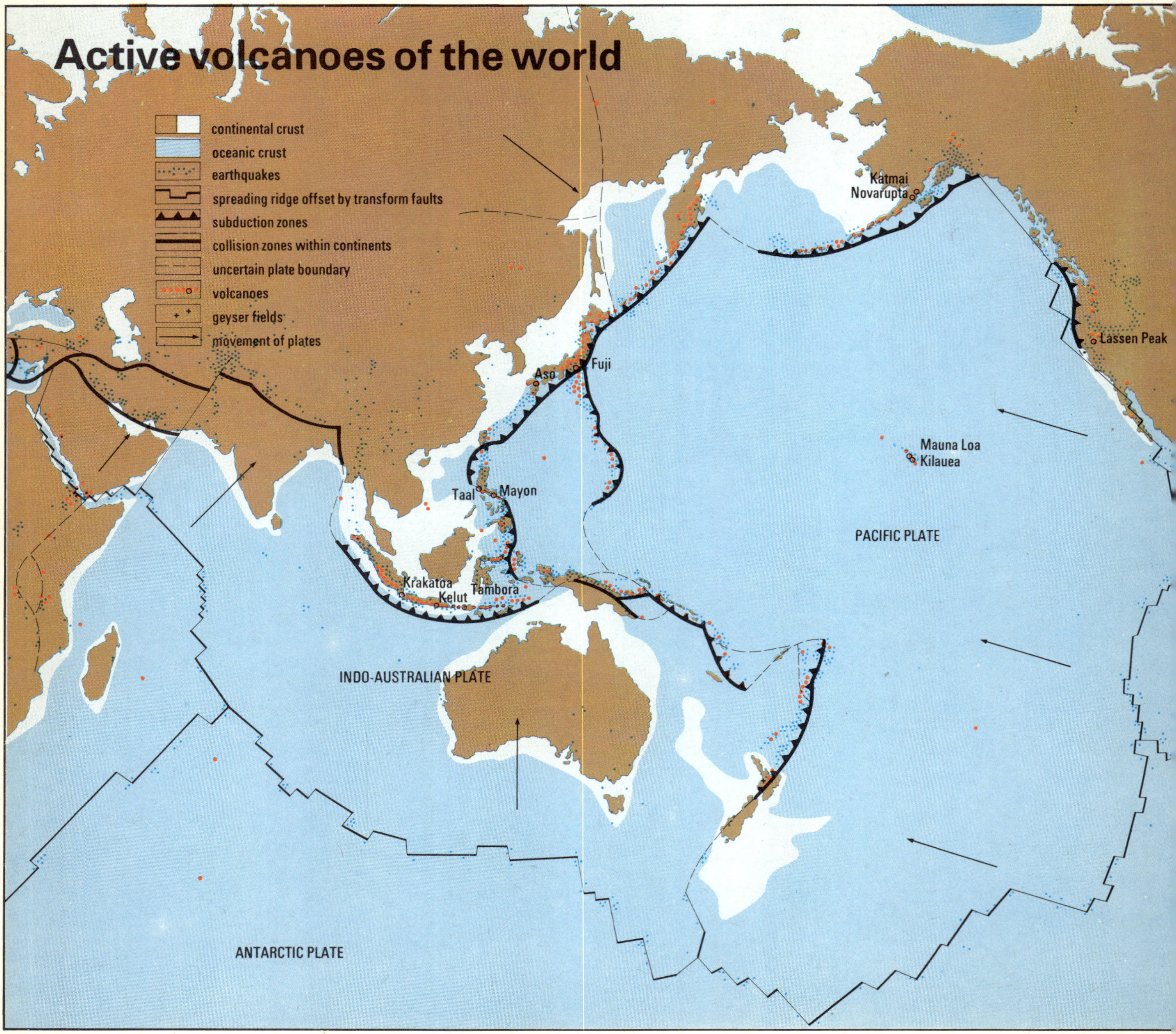

54 Active volcanoes in relation to the plate structure of the Earth's crust

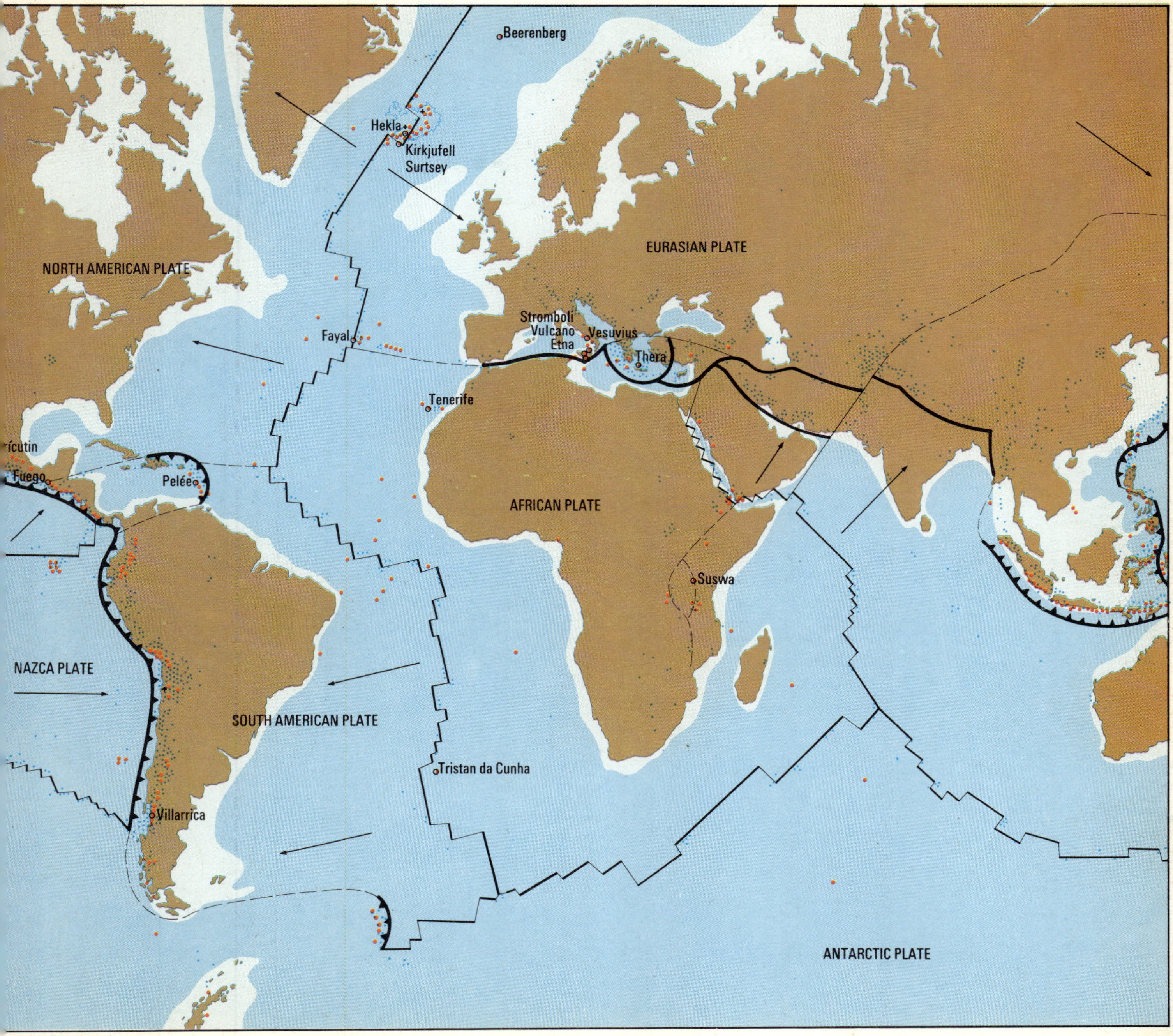

Beerenberg
Hekla
Kirkjufell
Surtsey
EURASIAN PLATE
NORTH AMERICAN PLATE
Stromboli
Vulcano
Etna
Vesuvius
Thera
Fayal
Tenerife
ícutin
Fuego
Pelée
AFRICAN PLATE
Suswa
NAZCA PLATE
SOUTH AMERICAN PLATE
Tristan da Cunha
Villarrica
ANTARCTIC PLATE

Magma

What causes volcanoes? The Earth is very hot inside, but it has a cool rigid crust which is a mosaic of separate, moving plates. Volcanoes and earthquakes occur in belts across the Earth's surface where these plates are being created and destroyed. Heat from the Earth's interior causes slow circulation of the solid mantle beneath the crust, allowing molten rock or *magma* to rise along mid-ocean ridges, creating new oceanic crust. Magma is again produced when this crust is forced to sink and melt under ocean trenches (figs 55, 56). The Earth was entirely molten, or very nearly so, soon after it formed. Although the Earth is largely solid now, its crust is still pierced by about five hundred active volcanoes. Mantle circulation occasionally results in the gradual extinction of a plate edge and the creation of a new plate outline, so that some volcanic areas become quiet while new volcanoes begin to appear elsewhere and chains of new mountains and islands start to form. Britain is at present geologically very stable, yet its rocks contain evidence of countless volcanic eruptions.

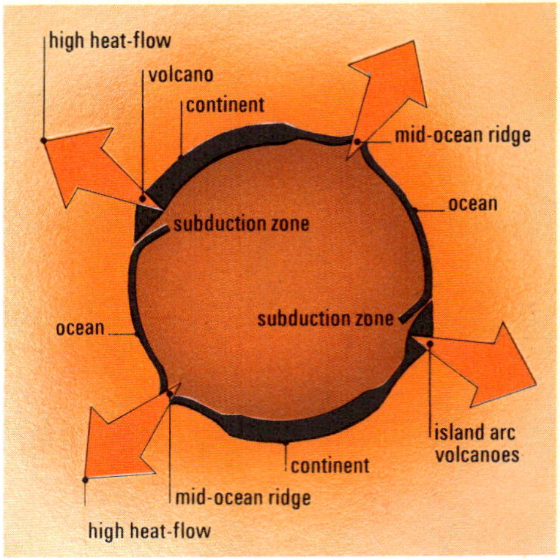

56 Earth's heat flow

55 (below) Igneous activity: magma generation and emplacement related to plate boundaries

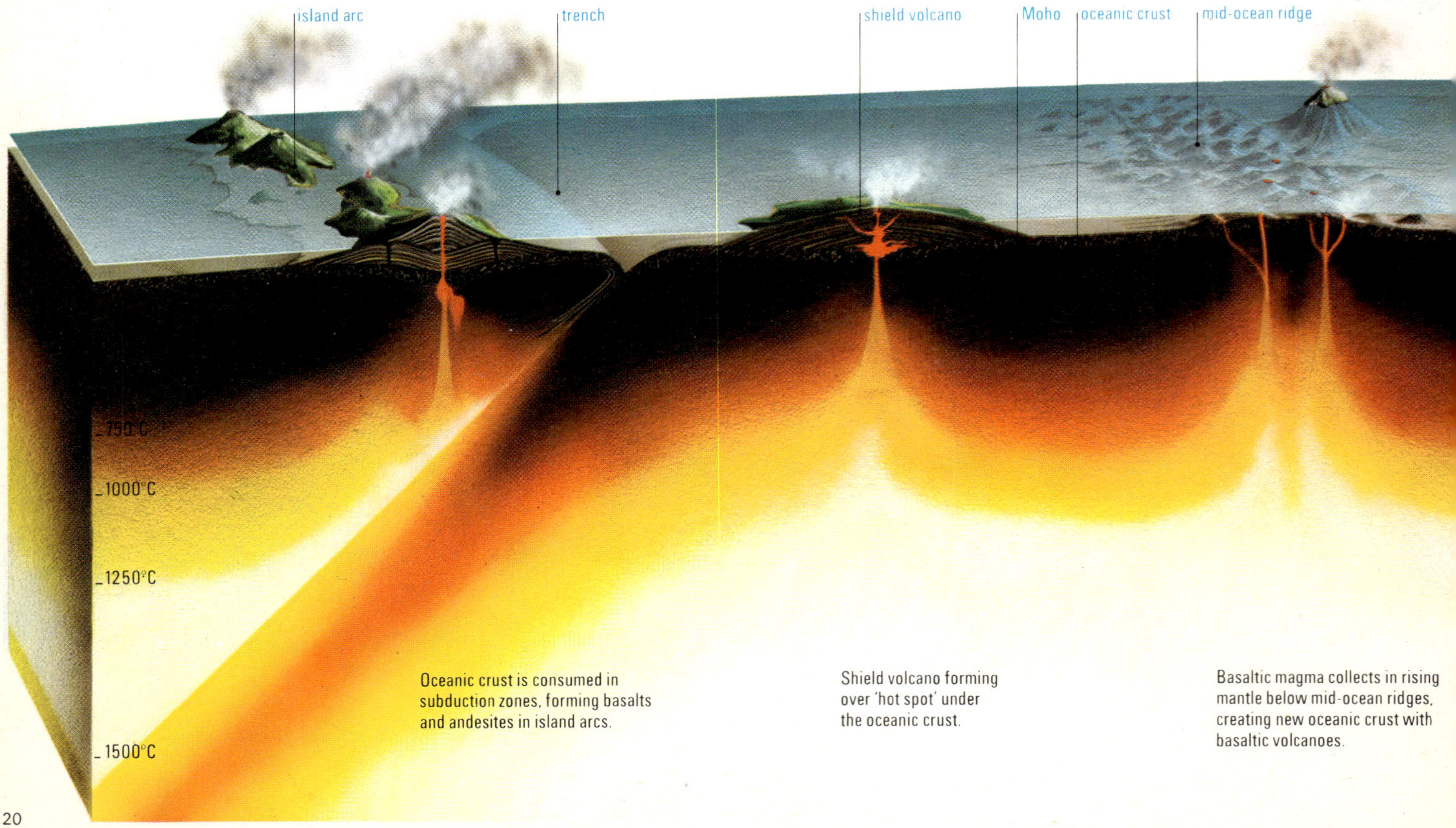

The genesis of magma occurs within the lower part of the Earth's crust and the outer few hundred kilometres of the mantle. The temperature at the centre of the Earth is conjectural, but the whole planet is certainly white-hot to within 200 km of the surface (Earth diameter: 12 734 km). Even so, there is no evidence of any world-encircling layer of magma beneath the solid crust. However, a layer exists below about 70 km down, where the temperature is high enough, and the pressure just low enough, to allow a very small proportion of the rock to melt, thus reducing its strength and 'lubricating' any movement. The crust and mantle above this layer act as a relatively rigid shell, broken into a jigsaw of shifting *plates* which are bounded mainly by the mid-ocean ridges and the zones of slow plate destruction, revealed as lines riddled by earthquakes and volcanoes (see world map, centre pages).

Mantle circulation provides both heat and suitable rock for the continual production of pockets of magma under these disturbed areas. This magma rises and cools to add *new* rock to the crust (fig 55). Different sites in oceans and continents are affected by different types of this *igneous activity*, the magmas cooling to form a great variety of *igneous rocks*. Some magma reaches the surface to produce *extrusive*, or *volcanic* rocks; much slowly solidifies underground to form *intrusive* rocks. Very large intrusions of magma cool slowly at depth to form *plutonic* rocks, such as granite. Beneath island arcs and mountain chains on continental margins, plates are apparently pulled or driven beneath the edges of bordering plates, to be carried steeply down into the mantle along earthquake-prone *subduction zones*, carrying oceanic crust, sediments and water with them. Deep melting in these zones gives rise to volcanoes erupting andesite lava, especially along large island arcs such as the Aleutian Islands, and also to the production of vast quantities of granite along continental margins, as in Peru and Chile. All these active sites lose more heat to space than the cooler continental interiors (fig 56), yet the heat lost through volcanic action is only one fiftieth of the total heat lost by the Earth. Heat generated by radioactive decay in the Earth's interior almost exactly balances this heat lost to space.

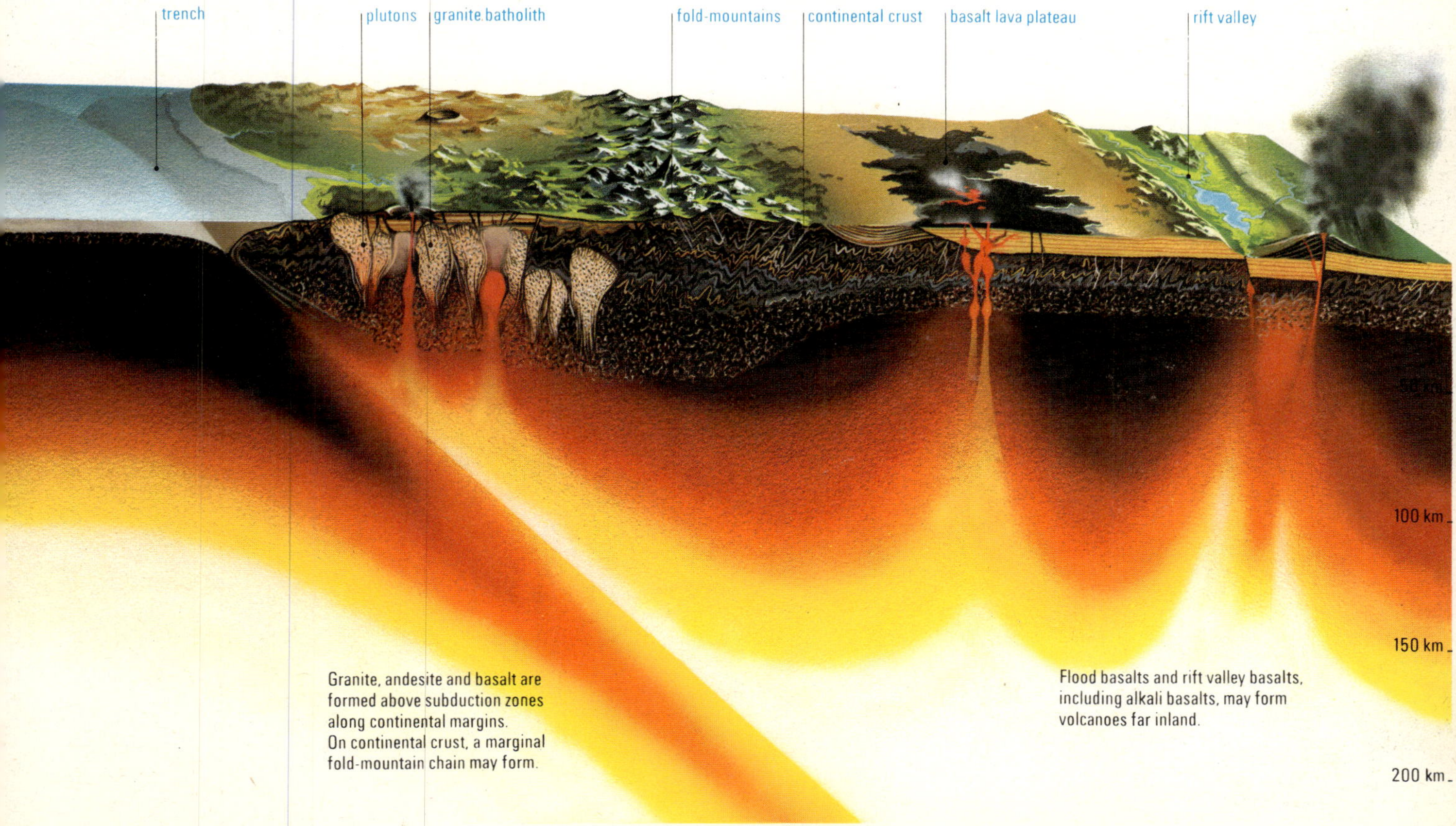

Granite, andesite and basalt are formed above subduction zones along continental margins. On continental crust, a marginal fold-mountain chain may form.

Flood basalts and rift valley basalts, including alkali basalts, may form volcanoes far inland.

Magma is formed as a result of large-scale movement of crust and mantle rock. Impelled by enormous circulatory forces, the solid, white-hot mantle very slowly flows, like ice in a glacier. Upward-flowing mantle reaches a level where its excess heat, combined with the drop in pressure, allows a small proportion to melt, aided by dissolved steam and other volatiles. Gradually, until the volatiles are used up, more molten rock gathers under the prevailing conditions of temperature and pressure. If enough is formed, the new magma rises away from a denser residue of solid, infusible rock. Fig 58 shows, reduced half a million times in scale, *basaltic* magma rising from its source in the mantle and erupting from a continental volcano. Hot, runny basaltic magma is the most common molten rock to appear at the Earth's surface. It intrudes at mid-ocean ridges to create new oceanic crust, forms the volcanoes and volcanic islands scattered across the oceans and floods out onto continents to form dense, fine-grained *basalt* (figs 55, 57). Partial melting at very deep levels, especially beneath continents, gives rise to ultrabasic magmas, such as those which produce *kimberlite*, a rare rock which carries proof of its extremely hot, high-pressure origin in the form of the occasional diamond crystal (fig 83) embedded in the rock. *Andesite* (fig 57) is formed along destructive subduction zones (fig 55) where oceanic crustal rocks, with some water, are carried down into the hot mantle. From these, andesitic and basaltic magmas are derived at over 50 km down; they rise to build up lines of volcanic islands along the ocean floor, parallel to trenches marking the crust's descent. Most *granite* (fig 57) forms in a similar manner, but only when continental crust is also involved. Enormous masses of granite may form when continental crust is partially melted. The granitic magma gathers and flows together, rising in a solid-laden, mushy state at relatively low temperatures, to form huge, blob-like *plutons* (fig 55). Plutons, despite their low density, tend to solidify and come to rest before they reach the surface. They break up the overlying rock into fragments (*xenoliths* figs 60, 61) which are gradually digested. The magma contains enough heat and volatiles to alter and mineralize extensively the surrounding rocks. The zone of alteration is called a *contact aureole.* Some granite plutons and their contact aureoles contain mineral lodes rich in metallic ores. Many plutons gather to form vast *batholiths.* Smaller amounts of 'dry' granite may form by separation from basaltic magmas. This *differentiated* granite often reaches the surface to form pasty lava and violent volcanoes.

IGS

57 Igneous rocks: basalt, andesite, granite

58 Ascent of magma

Solidified magma is called igneous rock. Much newly-formed magma already contains solid materials. As the magma cools, minerals crystallize out of the molten rock like ice from water, different minerals 'freezing' at different temperatures. The mineral content of the rock depends on the composition of the original magma and on what happens to it on cooling. The slower the magma cools, the larger the mineral crystals tend to grow. Sudden cooling of magma gives its molecules no chance to form crystals, so glass forms instead (fig 5b). Rocks of many different varieties and textures can form, even from the same kind of magma. This is due to different cooling rates (fig 59 shows two rocks which crystallized at different rates from basaltic magma), sudden volcanic extrusion, or incorporation and melting of surrounding rocks (figs 60, 61). Cooling magma may also lose its early-formed crystals which settle like snow, leaving the magma depleted in certain constituents. It thus becomes *differentiated*, that is, cools to form rocks which differ from any that might have formed directly from the original magma. Layers of accumulated crystals (fig 62) are sometimes seen to form 'strata' of igneous rock (figs 63, 64). Although differentiation tends to affect all magmas, newly-formed crystals usually settle too slowly to modify significantly the compositon of the magma before it solidifies. The new mineral crystals become unstable on cooling and are chemically altered by the remaining liquid. Slow cooling may allow a succession of minerals to form, but the overall composition of the magma (liquid + crystals) remains virtually unchanged.

59 Basalt (above) and gabbro. Natural size

IGS

60 Xenoliths in granite, Peruvian Andes

E.J.COBBING, IGS

61 Xenolith in polished granite

IGS

62 Cumulate rock

IGS

63 Layered rock

IGS

64 Igneous layering, Greenland

J.MYERS

Magma intrudes into the crust largely by sheer force shouldering apart the rocks. Solid rock is also disintegrated by magma into blocks *(xenoliths)*, most of which are melted or chemically digested by the magma. This process is called *stoping.* Some magmas, especially those formed at great depths, rise rapidly through the crust by a process of *fluidisation*, whereby the magma drills its way up as a turbulent mixture of hot gas and solid fragments.

65 Shapes taken by masses of molten rock (igneous intrusions) that have cooled underground

Intrusions of magma cool underground (fig 65) to form igneous rocks which are seen at the Earth's surface only if erosion removes the overlying rock. Intrusions are commonly revealed in prominent landmarks exemplified by the *plug*, or infilled conduit of an old volcano, in fig 66. *Dykes* are steep, sheet-like intrusions, varying in thickness from a few millimetres to tens of metres, which have cooled in tension fissures traversing the crust (fig 67). Many basaltic volcanoes are fed through fissures, which remain as dykes of basalt or the rather coarser *dolerite*. *Sills* are sheets which follow the bedding of strata and are relatively flat-lying (fig 68); less fluid magma may form the rarer, blister-like variant known as a *laccolith* (fig 69). Large, deep intrusions or *magma-chambers* act as reservoirs which feed volcanoes. They are occasionally uncovered by erosion; the top of one such differentiated granite intrusion, surrounded by basalt, is seen in fig 70. Deep sill-like masses of *gabbro* make up huge complex intrusions in some continental areas. Some of these, tens of kilometres across, and hundreds of metres thick, are highly differentiated, with granitic top layers and heavy iron- and magnesium-rich lower layers. Deep-seated masses of granitic magma may rise as huge blobs, like oil in water, to solidify within a few kilometres of the surface. These *plutons*, many kilometres across, may gather over millions of years to form single, vast *batholiths* (fig 55) some reaching over a thousand kilometres in length. A small part of the top of the Andean Batholith, where erosion has bitten deep, is shown in fig 71.

WARD'S

66 **Volcanic plug, Shiprock, New Mexico**

WARD'S

68 **Sill of black dolerite, Nipigon, Ontario**

G.P.L.WALKER

70 **Magma chamber (pale), Slaufrudal, Iceland**

F.W.DUNNING, IGS

67 **Dyke, Loch Cluanie, Scottish Highlands**

G.A.MACDONALD, USGS

69 **Laccolith, Uwekahuna, Kilauea, Hawaii**

E.J.COBBING, IGS

71 **Batholith roof, Peruvian Andes**

Igneous rocks in Britain have been produced in great variety in association with mountain-building, sea-floor spreading and crustal tension at various times in the geological past. Today, no active volcanoes are closer than Iceland and Italy; the youngest igneous rocks in Britain are about 50 million years old. The oldest rocks still recognisably igneous are over 2700 million years old. Erosion has cut into thousands of intrusions and volcanic formations which originated during this span of time. They range in extent from local ash layers a few millimetres thick to the 300km-long, 45km-wide granite batholith of South-West England. This huge mass, reaching from Dartmoor to beyond the Scilly Isles, was formed when the Hercynian mountain chain was built, at about the same time as the eruption of the Exeter volcanoes in South Devon and the intrusion of the Great Whin Sill in northern England, around 290 million years ago. The contact of the granite with surrounding altered rocks is shown in fig 72. Britain's most numerous large intrusions, exemplified by the Cairngorm granite, were emplaced about 400 million years ago, during the building of the Caledonian mountain chain. Ashes and lavas from volcanoes of this period form mountainous terrain like Ben Nevis, Glen Coe, the Ochils and Cheviots. A large volume of volcanic rock remains from the most recent episode of magma genesis, 70 to 50 million years ago, along a belt running through Northern Ireland and the Inner Hebrides. Massive shield volcanoes, floods of basalt lava (fig 73), granite intrusions and swarms of dykes formed during this time have all been cut down by erosion. Evidence of older volcanic eruption is visible in many other places. Numerous small outcrops in the Midlands contain volcanic rocks up to 1000 million years old, while the many more recent examples include the 450 million year old rocks of Snowdon (figs 29, 74) and the Lake District (fig 75), 390 million year old basalt and rhyolite lavas in the volcanic caldera cut by the road through Glen Coe, and numerous outcrops of Carboniferous lavas and ashes in the Midland Valley of Scotland. In Edinburgh, the remains of a Carboniferous volcano are still to be seen (fig 76).

R.H.ROBERTS, IGS

72 Contact of granite with country rock, Porthmeor, Cornwall

IGS

74 Snowdon, made from lavas and hardened volcanic ash

E.A.JOBBINS, IGS

73 Lava-flow with columnar cooling joints, Staffa, Inner Hebrides

R.H.ROBERTS, IGS

75 Bedded volcanic ash, Striding Edge, Westmorland

The Edinburgh volcano

Central Edinburgh is the site of a volcano which was active 325 million years ago. It is reconstructed here over the rugged crags of Arthur's Seat, showing the island formed by the volcano during its active life. After the close of its activity, the basalt lava and ash cone of the Edinburgh volcano was slowly buried under thousands of feet of sediment. Crustal movements eventually caused gentle folding, leaving the volcano tilted at an angle of 25°, while the area, including the volcano itself, was sliced into huge displaced blocks. Erosion of overlying rocks during slow uplift in the area has now exposed the broken and tilted volcano, and worn away its upper slopes. The resistant vent plugs, full of lava and agglomerate, remain as the most prominent landmarks. Although Arthur's Seat is only one of thousands of volcanic sites in Scotland alone, it is particularly interesting because it has been relatively recently exposed to erosion, just enough to reveal a variety of volcanic features which disclose the relationship between the present topography and the original volcano.

76 View of Edinburgh with reconstruction of the Carboniferous volcano of Arthur's Seat

Destructiveness of volcanoes

Prediction of volcanic activity may reduce or prevent loss of life, but little can be done to control damage to immovable property. Attempts to divert lava-flows include the use of water hoses to build a solid wall of cooled lava and bombing the sides to split a flow into multiple flows. During the 1971 eruption of Etna, vineyards, roads and houses were overrun by lava (fig 77); nothing could be done to prevent this since diversion of lava-flows is illegal in Sicily. Lava flows and thick blankets of scoria kill agricultural land for many years; the rate of recovery is fast in wet tropical areas but very slow in harsh climates – large areas of Iceland have remained desert for centuries. A lava-flow in fig 79 is covering an area previously scoured by a mud-flow of melted snow and ash which destroyed a sawmill and killed the workers. Both lava-flow and mud-flow originated from a fissure (still smoking) high on the flank of Villarrica. The most destructive eruptions are large explosive ashy eruptions, ash-flows and mud-flows. Mortality in these eruptions is related to population density, the highest recorded death-tolls being in Indonesia. During the 1815 Tambora eruption, 12 000 people died, but subsequently 70 000 perished through disease and famine which followed the eruption. To minimise the mud-flow hazard at Kelut, Java, a series of tunnels was built (fig 78) to drain the crater lake. The much-reduced lake evaporated at the onset of eruption in 1951 and there were no mud-flows.

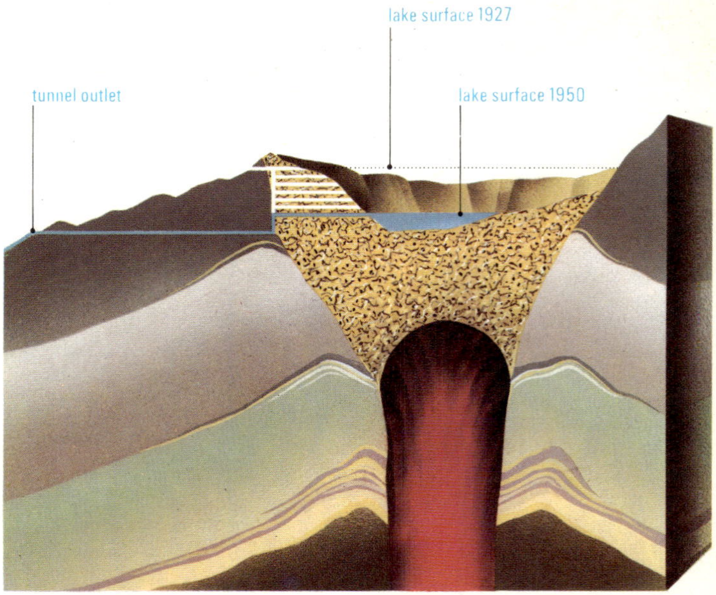

78 System of tunnels at Kelut, Java, to drain the crater lake

G.P.L.WALKER

77 Lava invading cultivated land, Etna, 1971

J.STEWART

79 Lava and mud-flow from Villarrica, Chile, 1971

Usefulness of volcanoes

As a counterbalance to their destructiveness, volcanoes have many uses. The soil derived from tephra is very fertile; in tropical areas, where the nutrients are leached from the soil by heavy seasonal rains, a light to moderate ash fall is a welcome fertiliser. Lava-flows which enter the sea build new land. Scoria deposits provide light-weight building aggregate: there is a scheme to build breeze blocks from the scoria of the 1973 Heimaey eruption for use in reconstructing the damaged town of Vestmannaeyjar in Iceland. Pumice finds a use as an abrasive, both commercially and in the home. Useful mineral deposits associated with volcanoes include borax (fig 80) and sulphur (fig 81). Hot springs have been used since Roman times for bathing and laundry, and the springs which feed the spas along the Rhine arise from late-stage volcanic activity. Fumaroles in the Valley of Ten Thousand Smokes in Alaska were used by explorers for cooking. On an industrial scale, natural hot water is used to heat houses, greenhouses and swimming pools in Iceland. Projects to generate electricity from the underground steam in volcanic areas are being developed at The Geysers, California (fig 82); Weiraki, New Zealand; and Larderello, Italy. Investigations are taking place in other possible areas including Mexico, Japan, Chile and Indonesia. Volcanoes are a good tourist attraction, and in addition, the isolated volcanic islands in the oceans are useful staging posts for air and sea travel.

P.W.FRANCIS

80 Borax, derived from nearby volcanoes, worked at Salar de Ascotan, Chile

P.W.FRANCIS

81 The world's highest mine produces sulphur, at 6000 metres, N. Chile

D.E.WHITE, USGS

82 Steam issuing at supersonic speed from a trial well, The Geysers, California

83 Diamond in kimberlite, with a cut stone

Minerals created during igneous activity range from common rock-forming minerals to valuable ores and gemstones. Minerals grow in cooling magma until, below dull red heat, they form solid *igneous rock* made up of interlocking crystals. Common rock-forming minerals, such as *quartz*, *feldspar* and *olivine* (fig 86), are occasionally found as gem-quality crystals. Others, especially *diamond* (fig 83), are, in any condition, extremely rare and valuable. Well-formed crystals are most likely to be the last-formed minerals in cavities or fissures. These are normally the most soluble minerals, or those that contain residual volatile elements such as carbon, fluorine and sulphur, and the less common metals like lead, tin and uranium which will not fit into the crystal structures of earlier, high-temperature minerals. These elements become concentrated in residual gases, which escape at the Earth's surface as fumaroles (fig 51) or in solutions which form deposits such as soda and borax (fig 80). These hot, high-pressure, mineral-forming fluids can permeate and alter the rocks in and around new igneous intrusions, especially the volatile-rich granites which are surrounded and intersected by mineral deposits and metallic *ore lodes* (fig 84). Similarly, large-grained *pegmatites* (fig 85) crystallize rapidly from water-charged granitic fluids. They often contain rare elements and minerals such as tourmaline, beryl and topaz, occasionally of gem quality.

84 Cassiterite (tin ore) crystals on pale granite

85 Pegmatite from Portsoy, Banffshire

86 Olivine crystal; cut gems (peridot); tumble-polished olivine crystals; olivine rock

Igneous rock is used in building because it makes a tough, durable and sometimes decorative stone which can be shaped, polished, carved or used rough-hewn. Its main use is in road construction and in building and monumental masonry. *Granite* and similar rocks have been employed in the past for basic construction of long-lasting and intricate masonry, such as in castles and churches (fig 87), and for statues, walls, kerb-stones and street furniture (fig 88). As a decorative stone, it is widely used for gravestones and polished wall cladding (fig 89). Several granite quarries still thrive in Britain; fig 90 shows a quarryman cutting stone with an oxy-paraffin flame which shatters the rock by thermal shock. *Basalt,* rarely used in building, is sometimes seen in drystone walls in Britain, especially in Northern Ireland. The Parliament House in Reykjavik, Iceland, is built of basalt blocks (fig 91). A great variety of British and foreign igneous rocks is seen in the polished slabs used on shop, bank and public-house fronts and on large, stone-clad office buildings, but the largest single use of igneous rock in Britain is for durable road chippings. *Volcanic ash,* when hardened by burial, is strong enough for use in building and cladding; green Lake District slate is an example (fig 92). Softer ash is used in some countries for carvings and building blocks (fig 93), while some ash is ideal for manufacture of waterproof cement.

F.G.DIMES, IGS

91 Parliament House, Reykjavik, Iceland

R.H.ROBERTS, IGS

87 Carved granite, Launceston church, Cornwall

IGS

89 Granite bank front, Brompton Road

R.H.ROBERTS, IGS

92 Farmhouse and walls built of volcanic slate

IGS

88 Cornish granite cattle-trough in Hyde Park

R.H.ROBERTS, IGS

90 Hantergantick Quarry, Cornwall

G.P.L.WALKER

93 Ignimbrite church gateway, Arequipa, Peru

Prediction of eruptions

Volcanoes are all different, so no set of symptoms can be used on a world-wide basis to recognise the onset of eruptions. *Observation* of individual volcanoes is helpful in predicting eruptions, and since the beginning of this century observatories have been established on many volcanoes. The observatory on Mount Etna (fig 95), $1\frac{1}{2}$ kilometres from the summit, was engulfed by the lava of the 1971 eruption. *Seismometers* are used to detect the small earthquakes, caused by movement of magma within the volcano, which precede an eruption. The earthquakes are continuously recorded at selected sites, but immediately prior to eruption scientists predict the exact location of the outbreak with the use of portable seismometers, like that in fig 96. Small tremors during eruption were unintentionally recorded in the time exposure of fire-fountaining in fig 97. Falling red-hot lava was not affected by the tremors, but the ground and the camera placed upon it, were shaken: consequently the film recorded wiggly traces of the falling lava. Some eruptions at Hawaii are preceded by a peculiar low-pitched humming or roaring noise; local residents call this 'hearing Pele' (Pele is the legendary goddess of Hawaiian volcanoes). The nature and origin of this 'Pele noise' is not known. *Tiltmeters* and electronic distance measurers are used to measure changes in the shape of the volcano which accompany eruptions. The tiltmeter record (fig 94), from Hawaii 1956–69, shows rising peaks corresponding to eruptions, and sharp drops at the close of eruptions. Movement of magma is sometimes reflected in changes of electrical potential and magnetic values (when rocks are heated above 600°C they lose their natural magnetism). The composition and temperature of fumarolic gases emitted between eruptions has also proved a useful guide to behaviour at some volcanoes. These observations and measurements are all supplemented by continuous satellite monitoring. It is hoped that an automated global surveillance system will soon be developed.

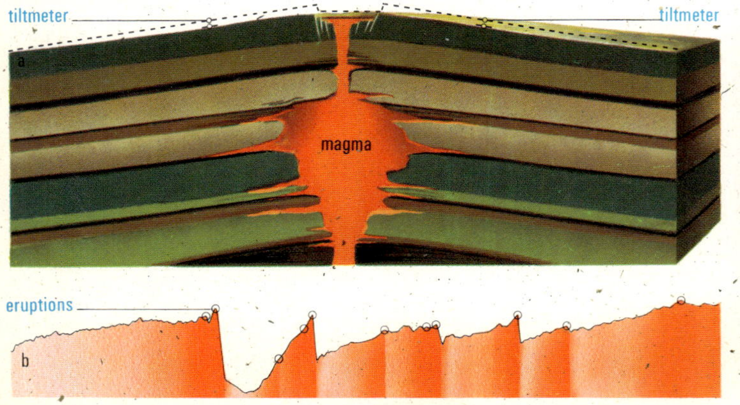

94 Tiltmeters measure change of volcano slope; (below) tiltmeter record

P.W.FRANCIS

95 Etna volcanological observatory engulfed by lava-flow, 1971

IGS

96 Portable seismometer for registering earth tremors in the field

I.FRIDLEIFSSON

97 Wiggly traces of falling lava due to earth tremors shaking the camera

Famous eruptions

Vesuvius AD79

In AD79, the volcano Vesuvius erupted suddenly and violently, overwhelming with hot fuming ash the Roman commercial centre of Pompei (figs 98, 100) and burying under volcanic mud the smaller, mainly residential city of Herculaneum. Until this eruption, the Romans had considered Vesuvius to be extinct: there were no records of eruptions and the cone was eroded and densely vegetated, with vineyards on the lower slopes. A violent local earthquake occurred in AD63 and damaged towns surrounding Vesuvius. Earthquakes continued for several years; today this activity would undoubtedly be interpreted as a warning of impending volcanic activity. The local population did not recognise this connection, perhaps because they were so certain the volcano was extinct. Consequently the great cloud which rose from the mountain at about noon on 24 August came as a stupefying shock. The cloud spread upwards and flattened out so that it resembled an Italian pine tree in shape. The eruption is recorded in graphic detail by Pliny the Younger in his letter to Tacitus, probably the first eye-witness record of a volcanic eruption. The details of his account have been confirmed by analysis of the rock products of the eruption, and it appears that this eruption showed many features seen in later eruptions (fig 99). It is often reported that Pompei was buried by falling ash and Herculaneum by mud-flows. However, recent research suggests that the 'mud-flow' deposits at Herculaneum may be ignimbrite, and it is probable that other towns around Vesuvius were also destroyed by glowing clouds. Some passages in Pliny's letters are remarkably similar to modern eye-witness accounts of glowing clouds. Extensive excavation at Pompei (fig 100) gives a very clear idea of how beautiful and prosperous this area was before the eruption. Excavations at Herculaneum (fig 101) are hindered by the fact that the town of Resina is built on top of the site. The rim of a huge caldera commonly attributed to, but possibly older than, the AD79 eruption survives on the northern side of Vesuvius as Monte Somma. On the southern side a new volcanic cone, Gran Cono, has built up since the formation of the caldera (fig 99).

IGS BY PERMISSION OF L.B. SANDERSON

99 Eruption of Vesuvius, 1774, from a painting by Joseph Wright of Derby

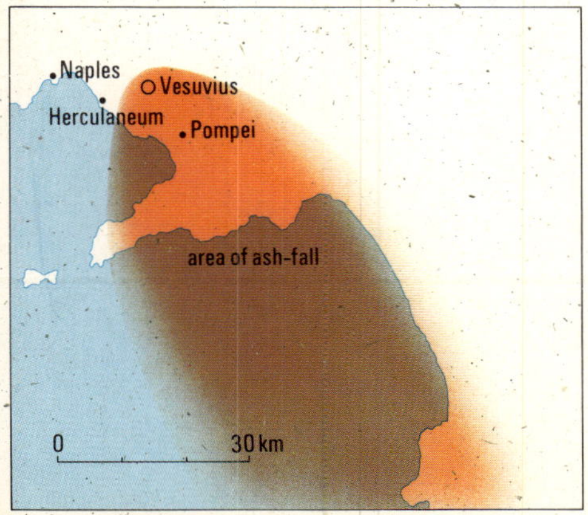

98 Vesuvius, with extent of ash-fall, AD79

P.RUSSELL

100 The excavated ruins of Pompei

G.P.L.WALKER

101 Herculaneum beneath Resina

Atlantis?

An enormous eruption on the Mediterranean island of Thera, in about 1470 BC, wrecked a whole civilization and possibly gave rise to the legend of Atlantis. The island collapsed during the eruption, forming a sea-filled caldera of 80 sq km, ringed by sheer cliffs of volcanic ash (fig 103). The cataclysm ruined the prosperous, Late Bronze Age Minoan civilization centred on Crete, much of which was devastated, probably by thick ash and enormous tidal waves. Greek legends allude to such a tragedy, but the eruption, and the Minoans, were otherwise forgotten until twentieth century archaeological research revealed their civilization. In 590 BC, during the reign of Tuthmosis III, the Greek traveller Solon learned from Egyptian historians how disaster had in ancient times struck the people of Keftiu 'far to the West' (probably Minoan Crete), cutting off their trade. Thus the idea of a lost island was born, and Plato, from about 380 BC, wove Solon's story into the epic saga of Atlantis.

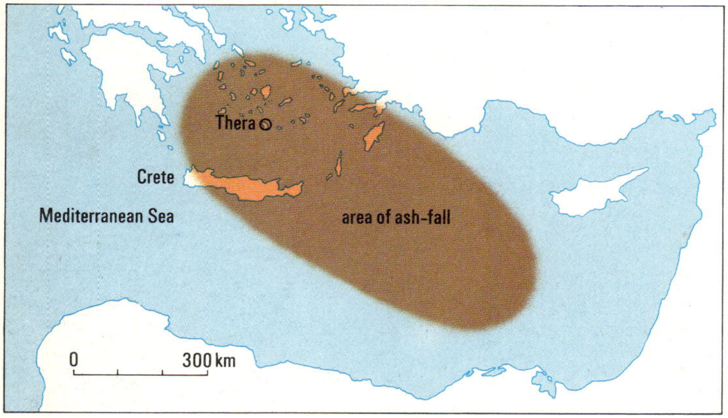

102 Thera ash-fall, estimated from deep-sea drilling

103 Thick, pale ash on Thera overlies the dark 'Minoan soil' level

G.P.L.WALKER

Krakatoa 1883

Krakatoa is a volcano of the same type as Thera. Both have a long history of small eruptions building up large basalt and andesite cones, followed by cataclysmic eruption and collapse, then slow renewal of the cones. The last great eruption at Krakatoa is recent enough to have been well documented. The first cabled news of the catastrophe is reproduced in fig 105. Effects of the eruption were world-wide. The culminating explosions, on Monday morning, 27 August 1883, were heard by people 4700 km away. Air and sea waves swept around the world; vivid sunsets, caused by fine ash, were seen even in London and huge islands of floating pumice spread across the ocean for months (fig 23). The deaths of over 36 000 people were, however, nearly all caused by the resulting *tsunamis*, huge tidal waves up to 35 metres high, which rushed onto the shores of Java and Sumatra, devastating 300 towns and villages amid a pall of darkness beneath an immense ash cloud.

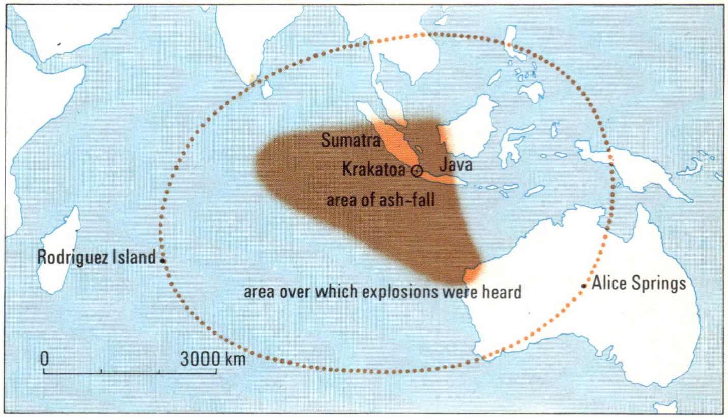

104 Effects of the 1883 eruption of Krakatoa

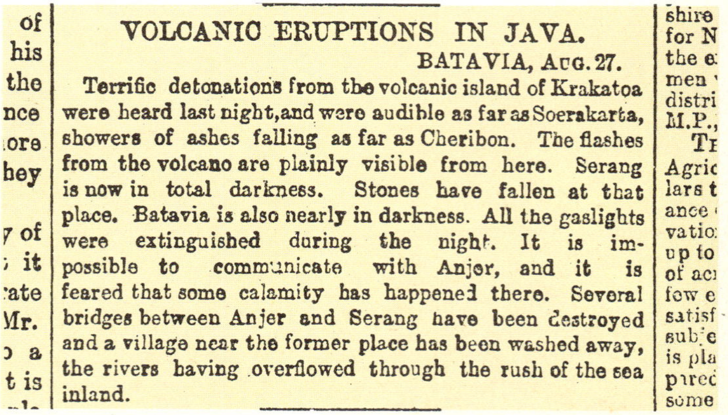

VOLCANIC ERUPTIONS IN JAVA.

BATAVIA, Aug. 27.

Terrific detonations from the volcanic island of Krakatoa were heard last night, and were audible as far as Soerakarta, showers of ashes falling as far as Cheribon. The flashes from the volcano are plainly visible from here. Serang is now in total darkness. Stones have fallen at that place. Batavia is also nearly in darkness. All the gaslights were extinguished during the night. It is impossible to communicate with Anjer, and it is feared that some calamity has happened there. Several bridges between Anjer and Serang have been destroyed and a village near the former place has been washed away, the rivers having overflowed through the rush of the sea inland.

105 Telegraph-cable from *The Times*, Tuesday 28 August 1883

TIMES NEWSPAPERS

Valley of Ten Thousand Smokes 1912

The Valley of Ten Thousand Smokes originated during an eruption near the volcano Katmai in Alaska. Three huge explosions, heard 950 km away, signalled the eruption of hot ash-flows which blanketed the valley to a depth of more than 200 metres. The ash-flows retained their heat for many years; percolating ground water was heated and escaped at the surface as innumerable fumaroles, the 'Ten Thousand Smokes' (fig 107). In addition to the ash-flows, falls of ash affected a much larger area: the nearest sizeable settlement, Kodiak, 160 km away, was in choking darkness for two days – it was impossible to see a lantern at arm's length. The magma of this eruption accumulated initially under Katmai volcano itself, but was erupted not through Katmai but through side fissures about 10 km away (fig 108) producing a new volcano, Novarupta. Withdrawal of magma caused cracking and subsidence of Katmai summit leaving a caldera 6 km wide and 800 metres deep.

Birth of Parícutin 1943

For many years a small pit on a Mexican valley farm puzzled the farmers by persistently reappearing after being filled in with earth. Soon after 4 pm on 20 February 1943, a fissure opened across the pit and emitted a small column of grey ash. After 24 hours, lava was escaping from the base of a 50 metre-high basaltic scoria cone which was rapidly building up over the fissure. Within a few months the new volcano had forced out the inhabitants of Parícutin village 3 km away (fig 111), and by June 1944, the district town of San Juan Parangaricutiro was completely destroyed by lava. By September the same year, the lava covered 25 sq km, and subsequent flows piled up on older lava. After two years, Parícutin volcano reached its maximum height of 500 metres (fig 110) and continued to erupt at a declining rate until, just after its ninth anniversary, eruption came to an abrupt end. Parícutin was the first volcano to be scientifically observed from birth.

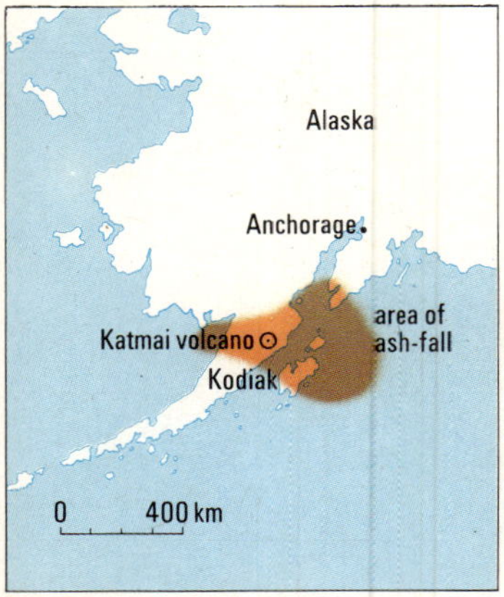

106 Extent of ash-fall, Katmai, 1912

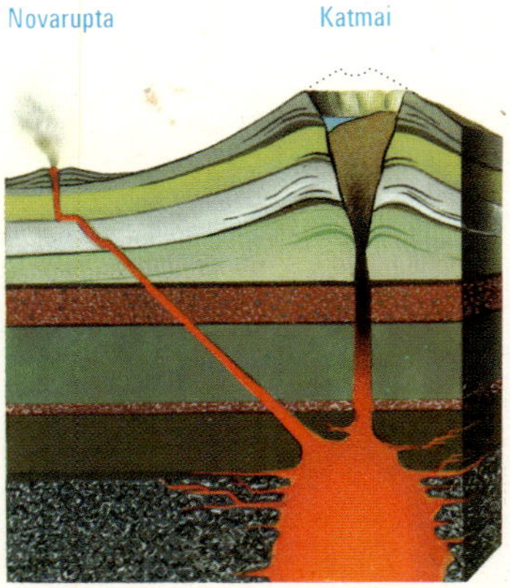

108 Magma movement, Katmai, 1912

107 Fumaroles in the Valley of Ten Thousand Smokes

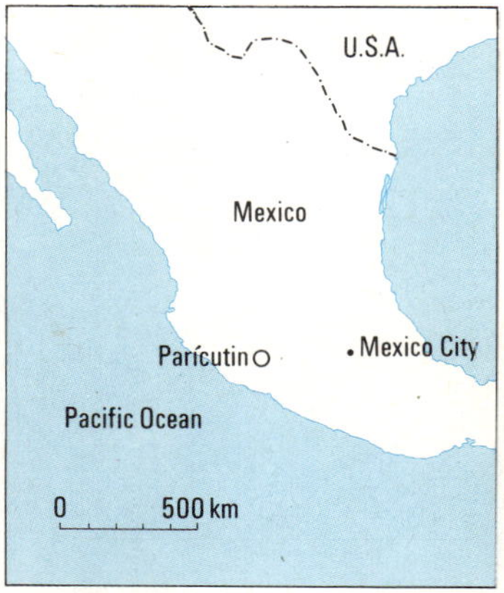

109 Site of Parícutin

WARD'S

111 Parícutin church in lava-flow

D.E.WHITE, USGS

110 Parícutin volcano after two years

Destruction of St Pierre, Martinique, 1902

The city of St Pierre and its 30 000 inhabitants were wiped out within seconds at 7.50 am on 8 May 1902, by a glowing cloud which erupted from nearby Mont Pelée. The volcano had been emitting ash and gas since 23 April to the extent that animals were dropping dead in the streets of St Pierre, suffocated by the poisonous gases. Even so, no order to evacuate the city was made, as an important election was imminent and the people could only vote in their home districts. Explosive activity in the crater increased, and mud-flows occurred on 5, 6 and 7 May, claiming victims in outlying areas. The glowing cloud on 8 May overflowed from a notch in the crater wall and travelled down the valley of the Rivière Blanche; it turned a sharp right-hand bend away from St Pierre and continued towards the sea, choking the Rivière Blanche with thick ignimbrite deposits. In front of the cloud was a rapidly-moving surge of hot gas and suspended ash. This travelled on undeflected towards St Pierre, devastating the city. The surge was mostly of gas hot enough to melt glass and metal; it left behind only a thin ash layer which blankets the background slopes in fig 113 like a thin covering of snow. Wisps of smoke still rose from the smouldering debris of the city on 14 May a week after the eruption (fig 113). In succeeding months, many more glowing clouds were erupted (fig 112), though usually they were less violent than the first. The last phase of the 1902–3 eruption was the growth of a dome and spine (fig 114) in the summit crater. This eruptive cycle of preliminary gas and ash activity, followed by a gas-rich phase of glowing clouds which relieved the accumulated gas pressure, and ending with dome and spine growth when the gas was exhausted, is a pattern repeated at many volcanoes.

IGS

112 **A glowing cloud eruption, Mt Pelée**

A. LACROIX

114 **The spine of Mt Pelée from the ruins of St Pierre**

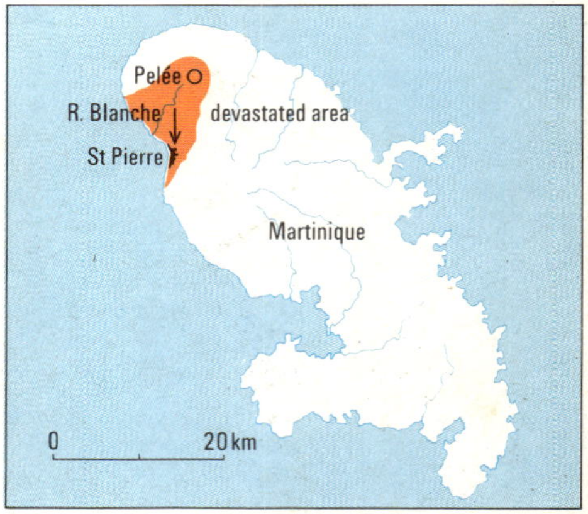

115 **Area of destruction, 8 May 1902**

IGS

113 **The smouldering ruins of St Pierre, 14 May 1902**

Further reading: *Volcanoes* by G. A. Macdonald, Prentice Hall 1972; *Internal Processes* S23 Block 4, Open University Press 1972; *Ice and Fire* by H. R. Bárdarson, H. R. Bárdarson 1971; *Volcanoes* by K. Wilcoxson, Cassell 1967; *Atlas of Volcanic Phenomena,* U.S. Geological Survey 1971 (20 wall charts).

The Story of the Earth, a permanent exhibition at the Geological Museum in South Kensington, London, explains the fundamentals of modern Earth Science. Highlights of the Story include a film of volcanoes in action, and a working model of a volcano.

116 **(opposite) Fuego, Guatemala**